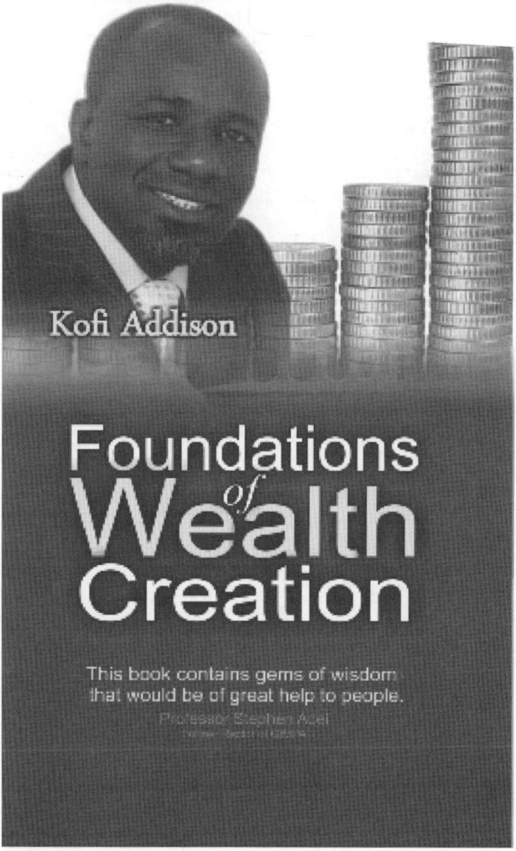
Kofi Addison
Foundations of Wealth Creation
This book contains gems of wisdom that would be of great help to people.
Professor Stephen Adei

Revised Edition 2013

All Scripture quotations are taken from the King James Version of the Bible unless otherwise indicated

ISBN: 978-9988-1-8774-3

Printed and Published in Ghana by:
GOLDEN IMAGES
P. O. Box MD 300,
Madina - Accra,
Ghana - West Accra
Tel: 233 24 4215411 / 20 8512971

Request for information should be addressed to:
Matured Leadership Consult
P. O. Box KN 1949 Kaneshie - Accra
Office: 233 302 662525
Cell: 233 24 4282015 / 20 7123121
E-mail: mlconsult@africaonline.com.gh
kofi@maximumbenefit.org

Dedication

To My father, the late
Joseph K. Addison
who's life have become
my guiding principles.

1942 - 1985

Acknowledgements

My profound gratitude goes to God who decided Ghana for me as my homeland and for the wisdom, strength, grace and inspiration given me to come out with this book to affect the lives of many people globally.

There are many to whom I would like to express my deep appreciation but only a few can be mentioned to represent all of them:

- **Apostle John Annan Adotey, Apostle E. N. Abebrese, Apostle P. O. Mankralo** for their spiritual guidance.
- **Apostle Eric Nii Aryee** for preparing the ground for the birth of this book.

- **Samuel Achiayao**, for arranging the book into a printable format.
- **Professor Stephen Adei**, for your mentorship.
- **Albert Ocran**, for inexpressible support.
- **Isaac Otieku- Boadu**, for your insightful input.
- **Jacqui Amy Iwu**, for your immeasurable time during the publication of the book.
- **Susan Acolatse**, for being supportive during the manuscript preparation.
- **Kojo Laryea,** for being supportive during the second edition preparation.
- **Kweku Gyasi Essel,** my good friend, for proofreading the book.
- **Agnes A. Yamoah,** My mum, for exhibiting an exemplary leadership in times of difficulties and also to my entire close and extended family members.
- Special thanks to the valuable listeners of **Maximum Benefit Radio Conference** for always finding time to listen and contribute to the programme every Sunday on Sunny 88.7 FM. God has richly blessed me with numerous influential academics, and

business executives, who have been with me through tough and challenging times. **George Buaful, Ato Sarpong, Isaac Yamoah, Samuel Lartey, Patrick Otieku-Boadu, Michael Noagbewonu and many more,** I cherish you all.

I will always remember the followings for their great impact on my life and ministry: **Bishop David Oyedepo** (Presiding Bishop of Winners Chapel International), **Dr. Mensa Otabil** (General Overseer of International Central Gospel Church), **Bishop Charles Agyin-Asare** (Presiding Bishop of Word Miracle Church International), **Bishop N. A. Tackie Yarboi** (Presiding Bishop of Victory Bible Church International) and **Bishop James Saah** (Resident Bishop of Action Chapel - Accra).

My lovely wife, **Deogratias,** who continues to love me though I give so much of my time to my work and to other people; and also my sweet daughters **Deoniel** and **Dianis** for understanding my calling, I pray that you would grow stronger in all things even when you think you are satisfied with your lives.

To all my beloved ones, I say may the Hand of the Almighty keep you safe in every aspect of your lives.

Foreword

The diverse range of economic and social challenges confronting the continent of Africa in the 21st Century calls for a new kind of understanding and the right attitude in order to guarantee success and longevity. The future of the continent is being shaped by a new crop of authors, motivational speakers and thought leaders who are challenging the status quo and presenting alternative strategies to break the back of poverty and ignorance.

In his maiden book, Foundations of Wealth Creation, Kofi Addison sought to demystify the subject of wealth creation both from the scriptural and business perspectives. He underscored the fundamental point that creating

wealth is a choice and anyone can start from where they are and, by the application of certain generic principles, go on to create wealth and enjoy it. In this revised edition, he adds to that knowledge through additional chapters.
Pastor Kofi Addison is more than qualified to write on this subject. Over the past several years, he has selflessly paid his due to developing young executives and teaching wealth creation through the Maximum Benefit Conferences: a series of seminars and radio broadcasts on entrepreneurship and personal development. His own experiences of poverty and deprivation in his childhood have placed him in a unique position to speak to the aspirations of those seeking to rise above their economic challenges and go on to live their dreams. I am confident that this edition will not be the last but another of many books to come from this great pastor and leader.

Albert Ocran,

Bestselling Author.

Author's Prescription

Thanks for choosing to read my book. This book has the potential to add to the knowledge you already have and also to make you achieve more with your life. But to get the best out of the book, please read it slowly with understanding and put its message into practice.

You would not get the real message of this book if you read it once. Keep reading it as many times as you would love to until you get the message as fullest as you want to have it. Even at that point, start reading it all over again until you are pregnant with its message. Each chapter comes with a summary to help your understanding.

This way the book will speak to your mind, your soul and your spirit as you put the message into practice.

Enjoy your reading.

Contents

"The poor do not need charity; they need inspiration. Charity only sends them a loaf of bread to keep them alive in their wretchedness, or gives them an entertainment to make them forget for an hour or two. But inspiration can cause them to rise out of their misery. If you want to help the poor, demonstrate to them that they can become rich. Prove it by getting rich yourself."

– Wallace D. Wattles –

CHAPTER ONE

Difference Between The Wealthy And The Poor

Why are some people wealthy and others poor? This is what I want to share with you in this chapter. Understand the fact that the way you position your mind determines the things that come to you. If you position your mind to be successful, you will be successful. If you position your mind to be poor, you will be poor because *"As a man thinks so he is" (Proverbs 23:7)*. There is something called poverty or scarcity mentality. The poor think of scarcity and those who are wealthy think of abundance. Therefore, there are both scarcity and abundance mentalities.

In this regard, it is mentality at play. It is not the difference in colour, race, tribe or nationality because we all have the same features. The difference exists in the mind. The way a wealthy person thinks and the way the poor man thinks create the difference. You were born with success to survive, and so far as you are on this earth, you have to uncover what God has hidden in you. In simple terms, if you are on this earth and you are struggling, know very well that it is your own doing, not God's. You have to create your own wealth, according to biblical principles of work and investment *(Prov. 6:6-11)* and by engaging in useful work *(II Thess 3:11)*.

This is what echoes in the minds of the poor: The world is difficult to live in. We create wealth from our minds and it is this very mind you use in thinking that the world is difficult and professing negatively to all people. You always give birth to things you are pregnant with. Therefore, if your slogan is “The world is difficult”, it would definitely be difficult for you, simply because that is what you expect and proclaim to the world. If you should get anything different, the world would be surprised because people know you by your word.

People who have scarcity mentality always have the mindset that everything in this world is difficult; and as long as you have this mindset, there is no way you can create wealth. Scarcity mentality says if you do this or that, it shall not be well. When people are moving forward, you would be saying that when we move forward it shall not be well. You hold your mind in your own hands, so you need to position the mind to suit your needs. Anything you focus on expands, so if you focus on your problems, they would definitely expand. You have the power to control the mind. Control it to your benefit and not to your own detriment. The word of God says, *"Be anxious for nothing but in all things through prayer and supplication with thanksgiving make your requests known unto God" (Philippians 4:6).*

You are what you think. There is something called the law of attraction, which means you attract what you think of. Whatever you think of is what you get. Immediately you think that if you try out a venture it would not work, it would definitely not work because what you think attracts. Your life is like a magnet. The world is full of many frequencies; demons are working, God is working and other spirits are also working. This can be likened to the radio. When you tune in to 104.3 FM, you would hear Peace FM. The question is, "Who tuned in the radio to 104.3 ?" The answer is obvious. If you, however, decide to tune in to 99.7 FM, you would hear Joy FM. Who tuned in the radio to that frequency?

That is how the mind frequency functions. What you tune the mind to is what you will get. There are so many frequencies around you. Similarly, we have Tigo, MTN, Expresso, Vodafone, Airtel and Glo as the current mobile networks operating in Ghana. But can you see them? You rather receive the frequency of the network whose SIM card you slot into your cell phone. In the same way, God has released success and wealth into the atmosphere. These are hovering around you, and only you can tune in to the frequency of your choice. If you tune in to wealth, you will get wealth. With scarcity mentality, all you think about is your background which limits you because probably nothing good has ever come from your family. I keep on telling people that one thing that never runs out in the world is wealth (money). Have you ever heard about shortage of money in the world? It is one thing that never experiences shortage. You have heard about water shortage, food shortage and the like. Everything runs short with the exception of money.

Do you know what money does? It moves from one hand to another and rests with people who can handle it well by way of investment. If you think that even if you sell an item people would not buy it, then surely people would not buy it. This is because you have attracted a *'do-not-buy-*

my-goods frequency.'

Poor people always think about scarcity. They are certain that the things they need are not there. Some may say that currently there are no jobs in their country of abode. Therefore they travel to other countries in search of non-existing jobs, only to realise how wrong they had been. You have created the world you are living in with the word of your mouth. The wealthy, however, have a different mindset. They say there is enough for everybody and therefore, they go all out to get their portions.

There is enough money to feed everybody in this world. You might be thinking that what you need is not there and therefore there is no need for you to expect anything. But the abundance mentality has a different story. It focuses on expectation. People with abundance mentality always expect the best in everything. In this context, the word expectation is a spirit and whatever you expect you receive, *"and he who seeks finds,...*

(Matthew 7:8b)."

A woman has to conceive before she can give birth. In the same way, you have to make up your mind to create wealth. You have to work with your mind. You have to work on the mind in order to achieve what you expect, and you would definitely get it. The abundance mentality is the spirit of expectation and expectation is not an expectation until you take steps or work towards it. Work is change. If you apply force to something and its position or situation does not change, you have made an effort but you have done no work. If you have not started taking steps, or working towards what you need, then know that nothing would come to you. Change your old mentality and profess that it shall be well with you. In the story of the restoration of the Shunammite woman's son to life by Elisha, the woman, no doubt, expected that Elisha could do it and indeed it was done for her *(II Kings 4:17)*. She believed that with the man of God's intervention, her son would be resurrected. She remained focused and confessed that everything was all right *(II Kings 4:26).*

Therefore, for everything that you expect, you have to work towards it. That is what we call faith. Faith is the embodiment of works. That is why the Bible says that faith without works is vain. If you do not work towards something, there is no way that thing would come to you. The evidence that you are expecting something is in the steps you are taking towards getting it.

Jesus had the same problem while He was with the disciples. The Bible says that one day He was walking with his disciples, when He saw a fig tree standing afar off. When Jesus saw the tree, He went towards it to see whether there were fruits on it so that He would pluck some and eat because He was hungry. The Bible says that when they got to the tree, they saw that there was no fruit on it. What did He do? He cursed the tree. The spoken word worked. He did not touch the tree; He only spoke to it. He spoke in a casual manner; not with power or passion and so many of the disciples did not pay attention to Him. He just declared, *"May you (fig tree) never bear fruit again! Immediately the tree withered" (Matthew 21:19)*.

The Bible says on the following morning while they were on their return journey, Peter called Jesus' attention to the tree which He had cursed the previous day. Peter said the tree was dead to its very root *(Mark 11:20)*. If you cut a tree, it takes days for the tree to die to its very root; but the word Jesus spoke killed the tree immediately and completely. Jesus looked at them silently and said to them: The power you have is not even for this tree but you can speak and you can move mountains. You have power to speak and move mountains.

When God saved us, He gave us power to change our lives. What Jesus was telling His disciples in this situation was that they were not using the power He had given them. We have what it takes to turn our world around. You can speak to your business and it would obey you. Say to your ailing business, “Do not collapse” and the business would bounce back. In the same way you have that power to create wealth. The power to turn your life around is in your own hands.

The mind is a blessing to some people whereas it is a curse to others. Some people have used their mind to create wealth for themselves and even generations after them. Others have used their mind to create lack in their lives- lack of money, good health, and good relationship with God and man. These bad situations have taken their righteousness, peace and joy away. The vacuum created is taken over by worries. They are worried about lack of money to pay debts and to buy new things. Their worries degenerate into depression and the end result is sickness or diseases. When they are sick and nobody visits them, they start complaining that nobody cares about them. Feeling sorry for themselves, they end up blaming God that He has not created them well. The pathetic part of it all is that the sickness brings more debts.

When it happens like that, the mind that is supposed to be used for creating wealth is rather engaged in creating bitterness. Persistent bitterness forces them to accept their condition as their fate or destiny. They unfortunately transfer this fate to the generations after them. They tell them, "As for us, we are poor people so do not mingle with the rich to bring any more problems". If their descendants are not careful to change their mindset, they also go the way of their predecessors.

This has caused poverty to run in and through some family lines. As the word of God says, they breed after their kind. The poor man unknowingly teaches his children how to stay poor while the wealthy man teaches his children to let money work for them. By so doing, they allow wealth to run through their generations. And the generation that comes after them is always greater than the previous one. You can see clearly that they are fulfilling the scripture that says the glory of the latter house shall be greater than the former.

CHAPTER SUMMARY

The greatest tool of the wealthy in society is the mind. The mind has the power that can transform our environment and circumstances, cause events to happen and attract money and possessions. The poor think of scarcity and those who are wealthy think of abundance. Therefore there are both scarcity and abundance mentality. The mind is a blessing to some people whereas it is a curse to others. Some people have used their mind to create wealth for themselves and even generations after them.

"Don't blame the devil for breaking into your life if you give him the access code."

– S.Whyte –

"As far as I'm concerned, the Devil has zero power! He can deceive, lie, tempt, etc., but he cannot make me do what I don't want to do. Hence, the Devil is an irrelevant nuisance."

– Unknown –

CHAPTER TWO

Don't Blame The Devil

Every sin you commit is by your own doing. I do not like talking about the devil because he is not in charge of my life. When you mention him, then you make him big in your life, so do not talk about the devil. Every sin you commit is by your own doing and so are its consequences. For instance, a woman goes to a man's house and the man then invites her into his bedroom and starts fondling her. The woman stays in there saying, "Stop this thing, please stop..." then her voice fades away. After he has had his way with her, the woman starts blaming the devil. The question is, "Who caused it?" The answer is obvious. If she had wanted him to stop, she would have taken an action probably by slapping him in the face or better running away from him. Rather, she was in his arms telling him to stop. Remember in the Bible, Joseph ran away *(Genesis 39:11,12)*. You sin because you want to. Stop blaming the devil. We have the power to flee from him or resist him.

In the same way, we blame the devil for a lot of things which he is not actually responsible for. People blame him for their financial problems, their inability to live a healthy life and other problems of which they themselves are the architects. I tell you, stop blaming the devil. You make him seem bigger and more powerful than he actually is.

Set your mind that you would be wealthy and it would come to pass. The only thing God can do for you is to help you by His Spirit and His word. God can never work for you. When you read the Bible, you will notice that God never does things for people. He helps you with wisdom and strengthens your hands. So Jesus Christ said that when the Holy Spirit comes, He would help you. When you read the Bible, it says that no matter how much a lazy person wants something, he would never get it, because God never works with lazy people. Laziness is not with the body but with the mind. So don't blame anybody for your failure, blame yourself. Yes, accept that you are responsible for what happens to you.

For this reason, put the mind under control. Think about good things and God will always be there to help you to succeed. If you have to fight, He will help you to win the fight but you need to move and act first.

CHAPTER SUMMARY

The devil is one of the most victimized creatures on this planet. All the fingers point to the devil for anything bad that happens to people. You need to confront yourself, and be matured enough to look objectively at what is happening in your life. Sometimes it's not the devil; it's you. For this reason, put your mind under control. Think about good things and God will always be there to help you succeed. Learn to take responsibility and move on with your life as you correct the mistakes or wrongs.

"Man was born to be rich, or inevitably to grow rich, through the use of his faculties."

- Ralph Waldo Emerson

"The real source of wealth and capital in this new era is not material things. It is the human mind, the human spirit, the human imagination, and our faith in the future."

- Steve Forbes

CHAPTER THREE

Laws Of Wealth Creation

Creating wealth is a deep statement, and therefore revelation is needed to comprehend its full meaning and apply it to your life. In this chapter, we are looking at the two distinct laws of wealth creation and money making.

The first law of wealth creation is the spiritual law. Human nature consists of the soul, spirit and the body. That is why if you are not rich spiritually, there is no way you can be rich physically. The Bible says, "*For what profit is it to a man if he gains the whole world, and loses his own soul? Or what will a man give in exchange for his soul?" (Matthew 16:26).* If you are rich physically but poor in spirit, what is the point? When we talk about creating wealth, there are four components of human life we should take into consideration; that is being spiritually, financially, emotionally, and physically wealthy. Therefore, if you have money and you are not in good health, then there is no profit for your money. This is the problem with many rich people in the world; they have more than enough financially but cannot enjoy their riches. What a pity!

The second law is the secular law of making money. This law can be described as an “Any how, any way you can make your money” style. Under this category, people do anything to get money. Remember, there is a difference between wealth and money. The secular law only states that so far as you have money, you are wealthy. Gradually people have misinterpreted the two laws of creating wealth and making money.

The spiritual law of creating wealth must balance

the four components of human life and make it complete. I want us to deal with the spiritual aspect because it is very important. Most people struggle to get money yet they cannot enjoy it because spiritually they are poor. God has given the basis. I mentioned earlier that wealth should be created in your mind.

Wealth, whether gained by spiritual or secular means, is difficult to create, but the secular way is more difficult because it comes with a lot of unbearable consequences. The easier approach may seem to be the secular law to make money. That is why some people would not stop at anything to get money, without considering the spiritual consequences. It is prudent that we apply all the four components so that we can create a lasting wealth. Abraham's wealth is a solid example of lasting wealth. It was enjoyed by his children even after his death. The wealth Abraham created was meant for all generations, including you and I, because he acquired his wealth through the right channel. Since it was acquired through the right channel, it remained for generations after him.

There may be some curses in your family but they should end in your time. You should enjoy the wealth and leave it as an inheritance for your children's children. Therefore, you have to go all out. For example, if you were playing football and the coach says you need to go all out, it means you must apply the maximum effort and give your all.

There is this management guru in America called Tom Peters who I admire so much. He once said, "In this life and age, nobody should give an excuse. It is the age that nobody should give an excuse as to why he or she is not successful." Tell yourself that nothing can stop you from being successful. Everybody living in this age should be successful, it is the age of success. So whether you like it or not, you should be successful unless you have made up your mind that you will not be successful.

There is this other man called Steve Forbes. He has a magazine called Forbes magazine and this magazine gives accounts of the lives of people. This man said that the billionaires in the world were few. Steve Forbes and Tom Peters made similar statements. The Forbes magazine writes about the richest people in the world. It says some years ago the billionaires in the whole world were only forty. As of 2010, we had over one thousand, one hundred and eighty-five billionaires in terms of dollars, not any other currency. What Forbes was trying to say is that people are getting money everyday so you don't have any excuse not to. It is the age of success, and if you miss this age, there might be no other time to be successful, for it is a technological age. The information you need for success is available everywhere. Formerly, you could not have access to this kind of information but now it is available. It is not the age when you should blame your father, mother or the economy. The economy has nothing to do with your success. The types of cars we adore today would not be of value some years to come. Just compare the kind of houses we build now to those we had twenty years ago.

This is the age of wealth creation, so if you are not yet successful, prepare yourself for a breakthrough because you shall be successful in the name of Jesus. New things are happening. Just look at the kind of sophisticated mobile phones people are using. The most important thing is to know the time you are in. Most people don't know the time they are in and are therefore behind time. The Bible says, “For lack of knowledge, my people perish.” The only thing you need to be successful is life and thank God you are alive.

Don't accept anything less. It is not biblical for you not to be prosperous. If you are asking for something which is not in accordance with the will of God, it will be a waste of time to ask for it. Whatever promises that are in the Bible are for you to claim because if you don't claim them somebody else will. There is enough money for everybody in this world, so if somebody has money, don't be envious because you can also get it. Just look at how banks are springing up and very soon there will even be one on your doorstep. That will show you that there is money in the world. There should be nothing like poverty because there is enough money.

You have to know the age you are in, understand it, interpret it and enjoy it. Things are happening in this world and you have to see them, understand them and interpret them or else you will not see success. But by the power of the Holy Spirit you should make it. Wealth is all around us and this is the age for you to be wealthy.

There is this famous man I admire so much. His name is William Shakespeare. He said, "*Some are born into greatness.*" Whether you are born into greatness or not, you can become great. It doesn't matter who you are for there is no excuse. Jesus Christ was born in a manger but He is now the King of kings and the Lord of lords. It doesn't matter where you were born, you can make it. One thing you should know is that you were born into greatness.

Do not ask for things that do not fulfil the scriptures. The Bible says *"Verily verily I say unto you, he that believeth in me, the works that I do shall he do also; and greater works than these shall he do; because I go unto my Father" (John 14:12).* Sometimes we make Jesus groan because we are ignorant, because everything you need to be successful is close to you. Your success is closer to you than you think. You are a miracle and that miracle must manifest in your life. Tell yourself: "I am too loaded to cry for money." Jesus said, *"He who believes in me shall do greater works because I am going to the father."* To be great, believe in Jesus Christ.

Wealth creation is not easy. The reason why most people are not able to create wealth is that they find it difficult, but creating wealth is possible. A research was conducted to find out why some people could create wealth while others could not. The findings were as follows:

1. Poverty had nothing to do with their families.

2. It had nothing to do with their tribe

3. It had nothing to do with their colour

4. It was not about their heights

The question then is why? The answer is their mindset.

Carlos Slim is a Lebanese who lives in Mexico. His parents migrated from Lebanon to Mexico. They went there with nothing, but this man now has become one of the richest men in the whole world. You can also make it. It doesn't matter your geographical location or background. Your life and your situation has nothing to do with wealth creation because you will be amazed when you compare yourself with those who have created wealth.

You need to break that mediocre spirit. Stop thinking about little things. Let your mind think big. Richard Branson was a school dropout but he is now one of the richest men in the world. Formal education is not a yardstick for success in life. If care is not taken, it could make you become a narrow-minded person, which could result in poverty. Formal education is good but it doesn't always make you successful, so you have no excuse. Most of the financial leaders in the world were school dropouts. Seventy-three per cent (73%) of the world's richest people are all school dropouts. Michael Dell was a school dropout and therefore education was not what made him to become successful.

We are in the age of knowledge. The world is full of talented people who fail because they know they have the talent but they don't have self-esteem. They have low self-esteem. You can go to school for as long as you can but if you have low self-esteem or you don't believe in yourself, you cannot make it. Low self-esteem is crippling the children in the house of God. If you want to die a poor person, you will die as one, but you should not die a poor person in the name of Jesus. Jesus Christ came to fight this mentality. The life Jesus lived on earth was not heavenly life; he lived an earthly life. He did not come as God. He came in the form of man so that you can interact with Him and do whatever He did on earth. People called Him the Son of God but He called himself Son of man because He wanted to show us that He was just like us and therefore we can make it. We have limited the strength, intelligence and ability God has given us.

Most people buy mobile phones for two main reasons, that is, to receive and to make calls. But the phone may have other features that you may not be exploring. The fact that you don't use all the features doesn't mean the features are not there. Similarly, you may have a computer in your house but may lack the ability to operate it to its full potential. This doesn't mean the potential is not there, rather it is your lack of knowledge which is limiting the functioning of the computer.

So if you are just living from hand to mouth, failing to know that there are other areas of the potential in you, then know very well that you are heading towards disaster. If you have not touched those abilities, I pray that you touch them in Jesus' name. That is the difference between those who have created wealth and those who are struggling because they have not used their potential to its fullest. The saddest thing that can happen to you is to die without achieving your aim. You have to leave the world better than you came to meet it. This is why in *Genesis 1:28 "... God blessed them, and God said unto them, Be fruitful, and multiply, and replenish the earth, and subdue it: and have dominion..."*

You may have all the potential but if your self-esteem is low, you cannot create wealth. You need to have high self-esteem, and with zeal, you will make it. Research has made it clear that about eighty per cent(80%) of hospital deaths are because of low self-esteem. The patients are usually not supposed to die but they end up dying due to their low self-esteem. Their low self-esteem makes them feel that because people are dying, they will also die. That is why you need to have a high self-esteem so that if you happen to be admitted to the hospital, you develop the conviction that you are coming back to create wealth, and enjoy your full life- span.

There was once an army commander who was on a battlefield and seeing that the enemies outnumbered his army by a thousand, he decided to burn down the ship they were travelling on. His subordinates didn't understand him. He told them that since their enemies outnumbered them, their only option was to kill them and then use their ship back home. The subordinates thought it was a stupid idea, but they succeeded. In some stages in life, you have to go all out and do whatever you have to do to succeed because you don't have any other option. The only option you have is to be successful no matter what happens. But remember, never use any crooked way; adopt means your society and the word of God agree to. If you are determined, you will do it in the name of Jesus.

There was a man in the Bible who was suffering and couldn't walk because he was paralysed. One day his friends heard that Jesus was in their town and rushed to inform him that his healer had come, so he would be healed. They carried him to Jesus, but couldn't have access to him because of the crowd. They could have gone back home without seeing the healer but they did not. Rather, they climbed to the rooftop, uncovered a part of the roof, tied the man with a rope and lowered him into the room. When Jesus saw him, He said *"I say to you, arise, take up your bed, and go to your house" (Luke 5:24),* and the man was healed. The interesting part of it all is that the crowd inside the room were amazed at how the man got in. This shows that success is determination in the face of fierce opposition.

There are times in your life when people and situations would give you tough opposition but you have to stand firm. Only then can you be successful. Those who have created wealth have determination. With men, it is impossible but not with God; for with God all things are possible. When He says yes, you don't need to find proof from anybody else. Jesus can change any condition, therefore be certain that yours is not an exception.

Some young men and women are lazy. If you want results, you need to put in a lot of effort. You have the ability to get the result but if you do not put in enough effort you will not succeed. Life is not for lazy people, neither is success for idle people. You can achieve anything so far as you put it to work. If you have God, then you ought to do away with all the fear Satan has put in you, *"For God hath not given us the spirit of fear; but of power, and of love, and of sound mind"* *(II Timothy 1:7)*

Poverty is not a friend. Somebody died because he couldn't afford one hundred Ghana cedis for medication. Meanwhile, someone else may be drinking in a bar with that amount of money. Poverty is an enemy. You must, therefore, do all you can to kick poverty out of your life. You need to move forward to be able to create wealth. If you knock once and the door does not open, knock again and again until the door opens.

If someone is sitting on your "gold" and you are not doing anything about it, then know that the person is enjoying at your expense. That person will run away if you act now. You must have a high self-esteem and tell yourself that success is yours, gold is yours, silver is also yours because they are an inheritance from your father. Make a move to fight and repossess them because poverty will not be able to stand your fierce zeal. God is about to do something new in your life; in fact, He has already started it. If you were rejected once, don't give up, go back and you will be accepted. Success is knocking at your door; just open and receive it in Jesus' name. Some uncovered the roof and had their needs met. So must you also. Enter wherever your success is now and claim it.

You must start thinking now about doing something new in your life. Before it rains, there are always signs and when you see the signs, you don't need anybody to tell you that it will rain. Therefore, don't expect anything else. Just look at the sign and know that something big is about to happen. You don't create wealth physically, because we are living in a spiritual world. Therefore start creating wealth from the spirit. You need your spirit to enjoy your wealth. When you create your wealth in spirit, you will be able to enjoy it. What we have done all this while is to build the inner man, which is the spirit. Whosoever God blessed was blessed in the spirit and the blessing manifested physically.

You need the anointing. I will share with you one of the main purposes of anointing. If you are anointed, it means you have been set aside for a particular purpose. Every anointing has its own purpose but I am talking about financial breakthrough. There are some people who repel money because their spirit hates money, and there are others whose spirit cannot attract money. Wealth is a spirit, that is why we say money has wings to fly. The anointing is like a magnet and it will attract finances to come to your doorstep. Believe it and it will work.

Somebody may be a very hard-working fellow but cannot create wealth because his spirit cannot sustain the wealth, so he needs God's anointing to be able to stand firm. If you are anointed by God, whatever you do shall prosper.

There was a man in the Bible, Jesse of Bethlehem, whose house God sent Samuel to go and anoint one of his children. Samuel asked the man to assemble all his children because God had directed him to anoint one of them as king *(I Samuel 16:3)*. When none of those who appeared before Samuel was the chosen one, Samuel asked him if the men were all the children he had. Jesse said that there was one in the wilderness taking care of the sheep. Remember that if God has identified you, no one can hide your glory. The young man was brought in. His name was David and he was anointed King. He was the one God had chosen, and he was set aside as king. He was carrying the anointing because God had chosen him from his brothers. God is going to set you aside for His special purpose and anointing. It will mark the beginning of your success. The success that comes from above is what makes you more than a conqueror.

Once you have been anointed, don't forget that your spirit has been blessed to attract God's goodness, which includes wealth. If you know the anointing that you are carrying, then explore it when you go to work. If you know your anointing and recognise it, you must enjoy it.

David recognised his anointing so he went to visit his brothers. The Bible says that when he went, he heard Goliath insulting the Israelites. Because David was anointed with power from God, he could not stand the insults Goliath was pouring on his people and so told him that he would kill him. Do you know why? David knew Goliath could not kill the anointed of the Lord who had killed both a lion and a bear with his bare hands. For this reason he made a positive declaration of Goliath's death *(I Samuel 17:17, 45-47).* I am communicating to you in the spirit; so claim it into your spirit. Whatever God has in store for you shall come to pass in the name of Jesus. Every Goliath in your life will fall in the name of Jesus. Your enemies will fight you but they cannot fight the anointing; it is the anointing that breaks the yoke and just as the anointing is of the Lord, so is the battle *(I Samuel 17:47)*.

Be serious therefore with whatever you are doing and tell yourself that it is unacceptable to die in poverty. With the anointing you will start attracting and enjoying wealth. If you don't enjoy wealth on earth, where else will you enjoy it ?.

The Bible states that when John had a vision in heaven, the angels were singing, so if you go to heaven you are going to sing and worship God because as a matter of fact, there will be no toil for the things of this earth in heaven. The only work is to sing and praise God. All the work is here on earth and that is why He has brought us here to work and enjoy the fruit of our labour. God is excited when the righteous prospers in His name. The Bible says in *III John:2 "Beloved, I wish above all things that thou mayest prosper and be in health, even as thy soul prospereth.*" Wealthy people always think about ownership - thcy want to own cars, houses, businesses and many other things, but the poor always beg. Wealthy people don't borrow. You will have and lend to the poor or give out as charity to the needy.

I travelled outside the country to look for someone I didn't know. All I knew about the person was his name and telephone number. I needed some items and through my search, I realised that I could get the items from Asia, so I went there. I got an address and when I called the office, a man answered the phone. I told him I was from Ghana and I wanted to transact some business with him. On hearing Ghana, he banged the phone on me. I called again, he said I was disturbing him and banged the phone again. I searched in the directory of the hotel I was lodging in and found the company's location. I couldn't sleep throughout the night. I reminded God of the money I had spent on travelling and about the fact that I always paid my tithe and so I therefore had to attract money. I told myself that I would not leave Asia without getting through with the business. I asked God to clear the way for me. I knew God had anointed me and because of that my cup would always overflow according to His promises. I also knew that because I had asked God, I had already received it.

I followed the direction to the office the following day and met the same man who had been banging the phone on me. I did not know him personally but I had heard of the name so I asked him if he was Wilson. He in turn asked if I was from Ghana. He offered me a seat. When I sat down, another man entered and asked about my mission. He had been told that I was the man from Ghana. After discussing the business with him, he said it was laudable. He added that he had just come from China, and that he was not supposed to have come that day but he did not know why he had returned. I told him it was because of me, for those people in the office could not have solved my problem except him. Could you believe that the contract was signed over a delicious meal?

So my dearly beloved, when you know what you are carrying, it will be manifested in your life. Don't look down upon yourself if you don't have it now. Only believe that you have it and pray that you have received it. God is alive. His anointing is like pouring petrol on firewood and prayer is like igniting the flame with matches. Therefore pray and call the fire from heaven to burn every darkness in your life.

God is desirous that you become prosperous, and have a mind that is focused on Him. Persevere with your mind and hand and through His manifold grace and blessing, increase in everything you do. Your gratitude and glory are always His.

CHAPTER SUMMARY

You have to know the age that you are in, understand it, interpret it and enjoy it. We are in the age of knowledge. The world is full of talented people who fail because they know they have the talent but lack the self- esteem to hone the talent for the benefit of themselves and society. Things are happening in this world, and you have to see them, interpret them and take advantage of the opportunities they present or else you will not see success. You need to break that mediocre spirit, stop thinking about little things, think big and remain determined even in the face of fierce opposition.

"Knowing others is intelligence; knowing yourself is true wisdom. Mastering others is strength; mastering yourself is true power."

– Unknown –

"You are the only person on earth who can use your ability."

– Zig Ziglar –

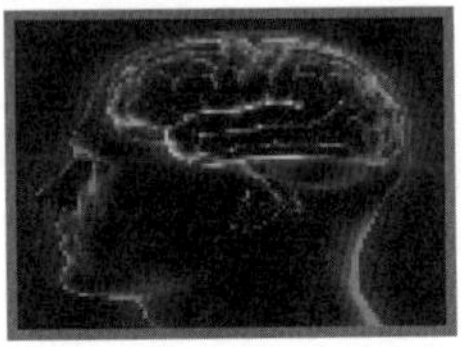

CHAPTER FOUR

Using The Power You Have

You create wealth using the power God has given you. You can turn things around if you first have the abundance mentality. You have to set your mind that everything you will do shall prosper. You have to say to yourself that whatever business you are going to do shall flourish. Move in the power of the Holy Spirit as a believer and do exploits in wealth creation.

Let us not allow the worldly people to be a threat to us, because we have more advantages over them. No matter their achievements, we can also have same but in a godly manner. We have something that they do not have. And that is the power to create wealth using principles or ways acceptable to God. You have the power to call things that are not there to come into being. The question then is why are you not using it? In my upcoming books we would tackle "Business Management and Investment Strategies" but first you have to work on your mind positively.

God does not save your mind in the course of salvation but you gain some power. Through the power, God gives you the means of controlling the mind. The mind is a battlefield of good and evil. It is up to you to decide to dictate to the mind. However, if you do not dictate to the mind, the mind would dictate to you and direct you either positively or negatively.

One thing about the mind is that it always fights you. Do you know why? Because the mind is lazy by nature. This aspect of the mind is called the conscious mind. The conscious mind is lazy. That is how God created it to be. Since the mind is lazy, you have to put the mind under constant control as it functions.

For instance, you may have a plan to do something but the mind could tell you whether to do it or not, or in what way to do it. You may either obey the mind or not. That means the mind conditions or controls the action you take to achieve the decision. The scenario for any achievement follows the same process and wealth creation is not an exception.

There are many who cannot go the extra mile simply because they condition their minds that way. You may picture it in this scenario: You are praying and the mind tells you that you have prayed enough and so you stop. But remember that those who pray for long hours also hear the same voice but they refuse to obey it. Remember also that if you do not control your mind, the mind would rather control you.

The difference between the rich and the poor is that the rich control their mind in any pursuit but the mind of the poor works negatively and in an involuntary manner. Be aware that if your mind controls you, then there is not much difference between you and the insane. This is true because it is the mind that controls the insane person and that is why when the mind tells him to drink even water from the gutter, he drinks it willingly.

The mind dictates to the insane person what to do and what not to do. Keep this in mind that the difference between the rich and poor is generally attitudinal. The mind is just like your hand, eye or leg. You have to tell the leg to move before it moves.

The fact is that when the mind controls you, you can never be successful and you cannot use it to create wealth because you are under the influence of a negative mindset. Each person decides what to do with his or her life because the power of the mind is in our hands. The mind must be put under control. The rich decide what to use their money for, their money does not control them. So if their mind tells them to invest and wait for a good return, they do so.

CHAPTER SUMMARY

What makes the rich richer and the poor poorer is that the rich control their minds in any pursuit but the mind of the poor works negatively and in an involuntary manner. Your mind is just like your hand, eye or leg. You have to tell the leg to move before it moves just as you have to use the mind to dream of useful or productive things. To accomplish anything, and to use your mind power, you have to know exactly what it is you want to do. To focus your mind power on a goal, you need to have a clear and well defined goal.

"Live your life from your heart. Share from your heart. And your story will touch and heal people's souls."

– Melody Beattie –

"Everyone is necessarily the hero of his own life story."

– John Barth –

"You must have control of the authorship of your own destiny. The pen that writes your life story must be held in your own hand."

– Irene C. Kassorla –

CHAPTER FIVE

My Testimony On Wealth Creation

I was born into a family of five and I am the fourth child. Figuratively, poverty tree was planted in our house. It was the poverty tree that gave birth to us and therefore we were its offsprings. Needs and wants were our bedfellows.

We lived in a dilapidated mud house in New Mamprobi, also known as Soko, a suburb of Accra. The house was built without a toilet and we shared a common bathroom with our neighbours. The mud house was half-broken and because the other half was also about to break apart, we used wooden beams to hold the remaining structure from collapsing.

I lived there with my mother and my siblings. When mice came into the room, we did not bother to chase them out because they were like co-tenants to us. We were so close in association with mice. Sometimes when you woke up in the morning and mice had bitten your fingertips, rendering it sore, it was no news because we saw it as normal. Therefore we did not even show it to anybody. This was the magnitude of our poverty. All along, my mother repeatedly reminded us that she did not want us to get into any trouble. In every situation, she echoed the fact that we were poor but gave us the encouragement that by walking faithfully with God, all shall be well. She made sure we did not mingle with kids from wealthy homes due to the fear that since we had no money, in case we accidentally caused damage to their lives or properties we would not be able to compensate them .

One day I decided that I would no longer be referred to as a poor person. I started to work against that mindset. I started from a humble beginning. My mother was by then selling roasted plantain, so after school I would sell some of the roasted plantain as well. I have sold coconut and plastic (polythene) bags before. I have also sewn the mouth of sacks for traders in the market and I have been a shoe shine boy before. Anybody who did the above jobs was assumed to come from a poverty-stricken family.

The moment I met Jesus, I knew I had seen the light. I knew I could not have Jesus and stay in poverty. I told my mother we would move from the dilapidated room. We were the laughing stock because we were poor. There was no help from anywhere because my father had passed away long before. He actually died in his poverty. The fact is if you die without having money, you are buried early. If you die in poverty, after the first meeting, you would be buried because the longer the corpse stays, the more debt it would be creating for an already burdened family. That was the way my father was buried.

I don't drink alcoholic beverages not only because I am a believer but also because people drink alcohol to their death.

My father was poor so I prayed to God to help me to outlive poverty. To that end, I always said to myself: "I would not be a poor man. I would do my best with the help of God to own the things my father would have wished to own.

I said to myself, I would think differently; I would think like a wealthy person. I worked on my mind. Change the way you think. When you change your mindset, you start acting accordingly. Talk and behave like a rich person and riches would find you. Talk and behave like a a successful person and success would find you. Resist any mediocre thinking in your life. Think big, dream big but start small. That is the road to wealth creation.

I broke the chain of poverty in my life by the help of the Holy Spirit. The first thing that I did was to build a house and it was the first ever in my family. That was the reason why I built my house very early. I was the first person to build a house in my family, the first to wed a woman and the first person to travel by air. I just decided to break all our barriers in the name of Jesus. If you change the way you think, great things would come your way. Never tell any one again that you are poor . Tell your friends that you are a rich person, so they better give you all the respect now. Change the way you think.

One day I told my mother that I was travelling abroad. Her first question was, "To whom are you going?". Guess what, I had just decided to travel to spend at least a day outside the country in demonstration that at least a member of my family has travelled abroad before. So I went abroad and spent six days. Now I travel as and when I see it necessary. That chain is broken.

You must be a pacesetter in all arenas of life. God would change your destiny in the name of Jesus. But first of all, change the way you think. Poverty is a state of the mind and if you break that mindset, you would enter into greatness.

It doesn't matter where you are now. I used to live in a dilapidated mud house but today, I live in my own house, "This is the doing of the Lord and it is marvellous in our eyes." It is possible with you too through Jesus Christ, the author and finisher of our faith.

I was walking with my wife one day when we had just started life and I told her that the following year I would buy a car and that it would be unique. By then I had an old Nissan Datsun 120Y car, which used to make a lot of noise when I was driving it. I told her not to worry because her new car would come soon.

The following year I bought a car, fully air-conditioned. On that day, I reminded her that the promise I made to her the previous year had been fulfilled. Years later, I told my children to take off the rubber covering our brand new car. You have to create the wealth by declaring it and you will enjoy it in the mighty name of Jesus. It is possible to create it. Whatever situation you are in now, please, do not let it hinder you. If you owe one hundred thousand Ghana cedis, do not think only about the money you are owing. Rather think about ways to get two hundred thousand so you can pay your debt and have one hundred thousand to start your own business or to invest.

CHAPTER SUMMARY

Do not allow your ugly past to influence your present and future. You have the power to break the shackle of poverty. It all lies in your mind. Change your story by changing the way you think. When you change your mindset, you start acting accordingly. Talk and behave like a successful person and success would find you. Think big, dream big but start small.

"But thou shalt remember the Lord thy God: for it is he that giveth thee power to get wealth, that he may establish his covenant which he swore unto thy fathers, as it is this day."

– Deuteronomy 8:18 –

"For what profit is it to a man if he gains the whole world, and loses his own soul? Or what will a man give in exchange for his soul?"

– Matthew 16:26 –

CHAPTER SIX

The Scripture And Wealth Creation

(I Thessalonians 4: 9-12.)

"But as touching brotherly love ye need not that I write unto you: for ye yourselves are taught of God to love one another.
And indeed ye do it toward all the brethren that are in all Macedonia: but we beseech you, brethren, that ye increase more and more;
And that ye study to be quiet, and do your own business, and to work with your own hands, as we commanded you;
That ye may walk honestly toward them that are without, and that ye may have lack of nothing."

This passage is a powerful scripture in the Bible about wealth creation. Creating wealth is a deep statement, and therefore revelation is needed for you to comprehend its full meaning and apply it to your life.

Now, let us go back to our central scripture: *"But as touching brotherly love ye need not that I write unto you: for ye yourselves are taught of God to love one another. And indeed ye do it toward all the brethren that are in all Macedonia: but we beseech you, brethren, that ye increase more and more;" (I Thessalonians 4:9-10).* According to The American Heritage Dictionary of English, "beseech emphasizes earnestness and often implies anxiety." Another word for beseech is urge. Urge is defined by the Oxford Advanced Learner's Dictionary as "to advise or try hard to persuade somebody to do something." Moreover, both words, beseech and urge, mean to beg. Beg is defined as "to ask somebody for something, especially in an anxious way because you want or need it very much."

This implies begging with both knees on the ground and with one hand in the other. What the Bible is saying is this: We beg you, this is not about prayer, neither is it about love; this is about your life. We are on our knees, begging you believers that you increase more and more. This means that there are people who are not increasing and even those who are increasing are not doing so more and more. So Paul is saying that they (Paul and the Heavenly Host) beg us to increase. Not just to increase but also to do so more and more. It also means that Christians should increase without ceasing. The scripture continues: *"...to mind your own business, and to work with your hands, as we commanded you; That you may walk properly towards those who are outside [unbelievers] and that you would lack nothing" (I Thessalonians 4:11-12 NKJV).*

God does not want us to lack anything. He rather wants us to increase more and more. When we increase, we would not lack anything. When you are wealthy, you would not lack anything. *"For ye know the grace of our Lord Jesus Christ, that, though He was rich, yet for your sake He became poor, that ye through his poverty might be rich" (II Corinthians 8:9).*

"How to create wealth" refers to how to tap what God has deposited in you. Have you forgotten that you were created in the image of God? "*God created man in His image, in the image of God He created him, male and female He created them" (Geneses 1:27).* This means God, in His own wisdom, created you to function like Himself.

During the creation of the world, God exercised faith by calling things that were not as if they were. In the book of *Genesis 1:3, "And God said, let there be light: and there was light."* In like manner, He created you to call things that are not to come into being. But since you lack knowledge, exercising this faith has become impossible in your life.

Remember that in Genesis, God gave us dominion over everything. In the New Testament, Jesus also states: *"Consider the lilies of the field, how they grow; they toil not, neither do they spin: And yet I say unto you that Solomon, in all his glory, was not arrayed like one of these" (Matthew 6:28b-29). In verse 26* of the same chapter of book of Matthew, Jesus states that *"Consider the birds of the air, they neither sow nor reap nor gather into barns, and yet your Father feeds them. Are you not of more value than they?"* You need to believe that life in Jesus is abundant and His promises are sure because the creator of all things has made it so. Remember that He gives freely to anyone who asks. Billy Graham once said, "Heaven is full of answers to prayers for which no one ever bothered to ask." *"Ask, and it will be given to you; seek, and you will find; knock, and it will be opened to you. For everyone who asks receives, and he who seeks finds, and to him who knocks it will be opened" (Matthew 7:7-8).* These are the assurances from God to you. They are to prompt you into action, knowing that it is possible in His name.

Human Nature After Salvation Revealed

There are two things that God did not touch after saving our soul through grace. The first is the mind. Your mind has not been touched by God. So all who are saved have the freedom of their mind.

God never saved your mind, and in creating wealth, you need your mind to do it. For this reason, the Bible says we should renew our mind. The mind needs to work, that is why the Bible is always pleading with us to release the mind in order for it to do what is expected of it.

The second is the body. God did not save your body. Paul again said that we should present our bodies as a living sacrifice, holy, acceptable and pleasing to God. This is because you have control over your own body and it is the main reason why you can use your own body anyhow. Whatever you want to think about, you can do it with ease. Even as you are reading this book, there are thousands of things running through your mind. Do you know why? It is because you still have power over your mind and body. So, it is you who decides the process your mind or your body should go through.

To create wealth, you need your mind. An insane person cannot create wealth. Unless you have a sound mind, you cannot create wealth. God gave us the mind to use in order for us to add value to our own lives. That is why you attend school for your mind to be trained. When learning a trade or a profession, it is your mind that is trained. This is because the mind has to work and translate knowledge into practical work. Indeed, it is in the light of this that Apostle Paul exhorts us to direct and polish our mind and its thinking process for excellence: *"Finally, brethren, whatsoever things are true, whatsoever things are honest, whatsoever things are just, whatsoever things are pure, whatsoever things are lovely, whatsoever things are of good report; if there be any virtue, and if there be any praise, think on these things" (Philippians 4:8).*

CHAPTER SUMMARY

Deuteronomy 8:18 says *"but remember the Lord your God, for it is he who gives you power to get wealth"*. God does not want us to lack any thing. He rather wants us to increase more and more. When we increase, we would not lack anything. Creating wealth is simply tapping what God has deposited in you.

In Matthew 6 : 26, Jesus said, *"Consider the birds in the air, they neither sow nor reap nor gather in barns, and yet your Father feeds them"*. You are more valued than they; God has His eyes on you.

"Always bear in mind that your own resolution to succeed is more important than any one thing."

– Abraham Lincoln –

"If A is success in life, then A equals x plus y plus z. Work is x; y is play; and z is keeping your mouth shut."

– Albert Einstein –

CHAPTER SEVEN

Liberate Yourself For Success

Change the way you see things. God is bigger than the things you see. God is there but you cannot see Him. If you, however, change your mindset, you will see God. At this very moment I want you to trust God that you can create wealth. Do not accept that you are a failure. Speak life into your situation. Look directly into the eyes of your children and prophesy into their lives. Tell them they would grow to be great men and women. Use your mouth to create what is great, noble and of good report.

When you read your Bible carefully, you will notice that God created the world by speaking. He said, "Let there be light" and there was light. Everything God created, He did it by speaking. He used His mouth to create everything, so any thing you want to create; you have to use your mouth to do it. The Bible says He created us in His image. If so, then we are like Him and if He created with His mouth, then we too should be able to create with our mouths.

God has given you the power to use your mouth to create your wealth. So if you get up in the morning, say, "I am becoming rich." If you are sick and somebody inquires about your health, you should respond positively that my health is becoming better. You would eventually get healed. Let me tell you the secret: Any time you speak, everything within you responds. That was why David said, "Let everything within me praise God." It is so because everything within you hears whenever you speak. It is a command you give your whole body. In the same way, if you say I am tired, immediately, you would begin to feel tired. Therefore say I am becoming rich and you would be rich. Let the poor say I am rich, let the weak say I am strong because of what the Lord has done for us.

There was a young man who was cautioned by his family that there was some particular meat they should not eat and that the day any member would eat it, he or she would die. A friend of his, knowing that this young man did not eat that particular meat, intentionally prepared a meal with the said meat and invited him to dine with him. They all ate without anything happening to the unsuspecting young man. The friend didn't inform him that he had used the forbidden meat for the meal. About a year later, whilst the two were chatting, the friend told him that he used their forbidden meat to prepare the meal they enjoyed that day. Immediately the friend heard it, he exclaimed that he was going to die. He eventually died because he believed it.

We have created the world we are living in with our mouth. Jesus became poor so that we would be rich. Behave like a wealthy person, and in that way wealth and success would locate you.

If anybody tells you that you are poor, tell the person that was yesterday, the times have changed and now you have seen the light. You can change your world by the way you speak. If you are sick, wake up in the morning and say I am getting healed. Some people may respond in the negative but tell them that you are already healed in Jesus' name for you know that you are healed. Henceforth, walk like a healthy person with an extraordinary grace to create your own wealth. At this moment, wherever wealth is, it would come knocking at your door.

The existence of the devil is real and doctrinal. But his schemes, strengths and weaknesses must be taught just as is done God's power over him and the fact that he has but a short time. Ours is to remain focused on God's promises in all dispensations through Christ.

Keep this in your mind that the moment you start thinking positively, goodness shall start coming your way. Greatness, breakthrough, success, and wealth would follow you in the name of Jesus.

CHAPTER SUMMARY

Wealth creation begins with what we think and say. Do not accept the fact that you are a failure; speak life into every situation you find yourself in. God has given you the power to use your mouth to create your wealth. Speak and think positively even during adversities. Also hold positive feelings or vibrations about money. By doing so you can attract wealth and money.

"The real measure of your wealth is how much you would be worth if you lost all your money".

– Thomas Jefferson –

"Only when the tide goes out do you discover who has been swimming naked".

– Warren Buffet –

CHAPTER EIGHT

One Source Of Income Is Not Enough

One concept that has separated the rich from the poor is the multiple streams of income. The rich have done something that makes them richer and the poor have not even made an attempt to know why. The concept of the multiple streams of income was developed by Robert G. Allan, the author of the book 'Multiple Streams of Income'. It urges people to have more than one source of income so that they do not suffer from the hardship associated with depending on one source of income. It also encourages investment.

The difference between the rich and the poor is 'knowledge and understanding.' The rich knows something the poor do not know. The reason somebody is ahead of you in life is what the person knows that you do not know. Knowing is very important.

The multiple streams of income concept makes the rich richer and the poor poorer. It separates the rich from the poor for the rich know that in order to stay rich forever they must create multiple streams of income because the more streams of income they create, the more successful they become.

Multiple Streams of Income (MSI) is a concept you must first know and understand if you want to be rich and to succeed in the years ahead otherwise there is no need for you to know anything about it. When you hear people talk about a concept, it is up to you to have the interest and find out what they are talking about and ask yourself whether you need to spend time to understand it. Your life will change if you understand this concept.

The difference between you and those succeeding in this world is their knowledge and understanding of the concept of multiple streams of income. It is the concept that changed the story of the Chief Executive Officer of Atlantic Virgins, Richard Branson. He currently owns over two hundred businesses. How can one person own over two hundred businesses? Bill Gates, Warren Buffet, Robert Kiyosaki and every rich person that you know owns a number of businesses. There is no successful person on this earth who owns only one business. All rich people own multiple streams of businesses. Why do you think they are opening more businesses? It is to keep them growing. You must understand the concept of multiple streams of income to make a big difference in your life.

How many streams of income do you have right now?. You have prayed to be more successful in the years ahead but you cannot realize it by saying it. You must understand the concept to help you make the money.

Firstly, you must have the desire for it. Secondly you must acquire the knowledge that you need because desire goes with knowledge. The Good Book says, *'For the lack of knowledge my people perish.'* You have the desire but you may lack knowledge. You can pray to God in church to help you to succeed with your business and believe in your prayers but now you must apply the knowledge to make it. You must know how to apply the knowledge right. If you are applying the same knowledge you acquired last year in this year, you will never see any difference in your life. Do you want to succeed? Do you want to make it big in life?

Robert G. Allan, one of my role models, says it all in his book.

Robert G. Allan: *'It is a tough business if you do not know what you are doing but it can be extremely lucrative and well rewarding when you learn the ropes.'*

If you do not know the business you are doing, then you are in a tough business and I wonder if you can make anything good out of it.

What is Multiple Streams of Income?

Multiple Streams of Income is not another business. It is a way of investing in various businesses such that you always have something working for you. It means you must not make money from only one business or job. Making money from only one business means you have only one source of income. Basically you must get more than one source of income. No successful person gets his or her income from one source. One source of income cannot sustain you in the years ahead. Whatever you are doing, you either create a Primary Source of Income (PSI) or a Multiple Source of Income (MSI). It is dangerous to have only one source of income.

An adage: *'Do not put all your eggs in one basket.'* The eggs belong to you but do not put all of them in one basket; in case anything happens, you will lose them all. I also say that if you must put all the eggs in one basket, boil them, at least.

How do you make sure not to put all your eggs in one basket? If you have one source of income, how do you create another source of income? For example, you can create one source of income every year, and within ten years you would have ten sources of income. If you have additional sources of income, it gives you another opportunity to grow and grow more. That is why every successful person understands the concept of multiple sources of income.

Different streams of income must flow into your big river. For instance, the reason why the sea is always there is that it never dries up. It is the source that receives different streams and rivers. Small rivers will dry up but the sea will always be there because it has multiple sources of 'in flows' that feed it. If you want to be very rich and grow richer, you also must be very solid and create more streams to flow your direction.

Your primary source of income is like the sea, so how do you create streams to help grow your primary source of income? You must create multiple streams of income to be able to feed your sea. That way it will always remain full. That is why multiple streams of income is very crucial to your success.

If you understand the concept of multiple streams of income, you will be so excited with what you are doing. Sometimes, because you do not understand certain basic things in business, it becomes very challenging and difficult for you to make it. You may be doing things that do not help you to grow but if you understand the system and the concept of multiple streams of income very well, it helps solve many of your problems in life. This book will help guide you to create multiple streams of income out of your primary source of income. You do not need to get out of your working environment to get into another business.

The Third Income

We have reached an age where we need 'The Third Income.' We are in an age where three, four or five incomes or even more can run a successful family to live the kind of life they desire, eat the kind of food they want or take the kind of holidays they want. Many families have never taken holidays before because their income is not enough to meet holiday expenses. There are certain basic things that you need in life that even two incomes sometimes cannot take care of. No successful person in this world relies on one income. We are not in the age of Andrew Carnegie where he ran only the steel works. Even John Rockefeller was running multiple streams of businesses in his time. These are some of the things that you must understand. It is not about you; it is about where the world has got to.

This is why the third income becomes very relevant, especially for families. It simply refers to the stream a husband and a wife can create in addition to their own two regular sources of incomes, probably salaries, if they are salaried workers.

The world has got to a stage where you must think of how to multiply your income. If you are paid ten thousand Ghana cedis or one hundred Ghana cedis or two hundred Ghana cedis as your monthly salary, you need to multiply it. If you live on two hundred Ghana cedis and you are paid one hundred Ghana cedis, how do you get two hundred Ghana cedis to live on within the month? How do you do it? How do you live a comfortable life? How do you save to go back to school? You would realize that you want to save but you cannot because the amount you make cannot sustain your living standard, so going back to school, for instance, is impossible.

Some people are going back to school because they think by doing that their salaries will be increased. Everybody is struggling to double his or her income so you see people rushing to school and it is very good. More universities are emerging because people are eager to learn now because they know it is a means of doubling their income. The same thing applies to you if you want to double your income.

You must understand that people are doing so many things to double their incomes. Do you want to double your income? Do you want the third income? Do you want to succeed in life? You see people driving beautiful cars that you also wish to possess? You want to live in a beautiful home because others also are living in wonderful homes. People are wearing nice clothes and you also want to wear nice clothes. People are eating good food and you also want to eat good food. You want it but the salary you receive at the end of the month does not permit you to have it. So how do you double your income? How do you get the third income? How do you get other streams to flow into your financial sea? How do you make sure that if this one is not working, the other will work?

CHAPTER SUMMARY

The multiple streams of income make the rich richer and the poor poorer. It widens the gap between them. For there is no successful person on this earth who owns one business; all rich people own multiple businesses. Multiple streams of income is not another business; it is a way of investing in various businesses such that you always have something working for you. Remember, many people are doing so many things to double their income and you can also do same.

" There is only one class in the community that think more about money than the rich, and that is the poor. The poor man can think of nothing else".

– Oscar Wilde –

"To live is to choose. But to chose well, you must know who you are and what you stand for, where you want to go and why you want to get there".

– Kofi Annan –

CHAPTER NINE

Make Money While Asleep

If you do not have the reason for possessing anything, there is no need to look for it. You must have a reason why you need this or that and why you want to grow and become better in life. Why do you want to succeed financially in the work you are doing? The main reason you need multiple streams of income is to be able to make money even while you are asleep. Every successful person makes money while he or she is asleep. Do you make money only when you are awake or also while you are asleep?

The difference between the rich and the poor is that one group makes money while awake whereas the other makes money whether asleep or awake. The money the rich make while both asleep and awake is what separates them from the poor. The moment the poor sleep, money stops flowing into their lives but when the rich go to bed, money keeps on flowing into their lives. Does money flow into your life when you go to bed or only when you are awake? Do you have to be there in person before you make money? If you are not there, can money not flow to you?

Is the money that flows into your pocket or runs into your account what you make physically when your eyes are wide open? What happens in your sleeping time? If you die today will money still flow into your account? You can never be successful if you only make money when you are around physically. If the rich die today monies will still flow into their accounts because of the streams that they have created for themselves. You must learn how to create multiple streams of income. If you really want to see your life become better, you must understand this concept. You must know how this concept works for it to help you to succeed in life.

If you are to go on retirement now, which is very important, I can assure you that the money SSNIT will give you cannot take care of you. If you depend on it you will die early. You need at least sixty per cent(60%) of the money you are earningtoday to live a comfortable life in your retirement. It is not about social security contributions; it is about how you prepare yourself for your retirement. What can keep you alive in your retirement are the streams you built when you were actively working.

If you are able to build streams at this stage of your life, in your retirement, you will be very excited because those streams will take care of you. Multiple Streams of Income is a concept that will help you to live longer. Research has proven that when most people are about to retire they die and others do not live long either while on retirement because of worries. It is more logical to focus on creating multiple streams of income than expect to live on the pension stipend.

Learn and get the understanding of the concept because there is no successful person living on this earth who does not understand it. It keeps successful people alive. It is not wise to rely on your job. Your job must help you to create another stream. It is very pathetic at times if one is not able to create multiple streams of income. Companies are downsizing and people are easily losing their jobs. The unemployed are more than the employed. You can easily lose your job if you are working in any organization because the number of application letters that come in when a vacancy advertisement is placed is very high. The young and energetic ones are really knocking at doors for employment because they go on the Internet and find job placement there.

If you want job security, the best thing you must do is to understand this multiple streams of income concept and build on it to give you peace of mind. Even if you are thrown out of a company, there is something that can hold you up a little bit while you look for another job. The inadequate salary or wage is making even those in employment look elsewhere for greener pastures. They want to leave current jobs because their salaries cannot sustain their lives and those of their families.

People are looking for opportunities so they are applying for jobs everywhere. Everybody is looking for an outlet because we have reached a stage where it is easier to lose your job and easier to lose your staff. It is everywhere so you can easily lose a whole staff over a period. You can easily lose somebody who is helping you to get to where you want to reach. You must understand the Multiple Streams of Income and get yourself involved in it. In this twenty-first century, one of the concepts you must understand is the concept of multiple streams of income.

The Good Book: *'The love of money is the root of all evil.'* Yes, it is true, but **George Bernard** says *'The lack of money is the root of all evil.'* The two sayings are both true in that 'love' in the first saying implies going for money even when it calls for partaking in a certain evil for the money to flow. Making money should be guided by acceptable principles and practices. I like what **Don** said, *'When a man tells you that he got rich through hard work, ask him whose?'*

Who told you that working hard will make you rich? Somebody says, 'I work very hard.' Everybody is working very hard but it depends on what you are doing. It depends on the concept that you understand. If you understand the concept of multiple streams of income, then you are working very hard because you understand what you are doing. The difference between the rich and the poor is that, the poor are working harder than the rich in terms of human power. It is not about physical power but it is about the mind power. If it is about physical power, the rich do not have that energy.

Donald Trump: *'Money was never a big motivation for me except as a way to keep score the real excitement in playing the game.'*

Warren Buffet: *'Investment is a game that you must understand how to play.'*

If you do not know how to play football, you cannot play it. If you do not know how to play the financial game, you cannot play it. For you to be able to play the game very well, you must understand it. To be successful, you must understand it. Study the lives of people you know who are succeeding in life. They are not doing one thing. They have other streams of income that flow their direction. Learn how to create the additional stream that will make a way for you to succeed.

Max: *'Money frees you from doing things you dislike and since I dislike doing nearly everything money is handy.'*

Money is very important if you understand how it works. If you understand the concept, you must apply it and spend more time and energy to build on it. You must understand how interest works. If somebody is working from 8a.m. to 5p.m. you must understand that system. You must understand why we work from eight to five. It is a system. That is why you go to work at 8a.m. and close at 5p.m. If you understand basic systems such as this, it will help you to understand the kind of life you should lead.

Robert G. Allan: *'If service is the rent you pay for your existence on this earth, are you behind your rent?'*

Allan is asking whether you are rendering more services to people or you are just giving out only one service. If service is the rent you pay for your existence on this earth, are you behind your rent? How many people are getting services from you? How many people are you serving with your life? How many people are you serving with your expertise? How many people depend on you to move to the next level of their lives? This is what Robert G. Allan is talking about. That is crucial for you to understand the concept of multiple streams of income. What are you doing in addition to what you know and do regularly?

There are three broad areas in which to create multiple streams of income. One area is the real estate, the second is the paper asset and the third is building your own business. These three broad areas are very crucial in building wealth and residual income.

The Interest System

You must understand the interest system in the multiple streams of income. The rich understand what the interest system is but the poor do not. The system that takes money from the poor is the interest. The poor pay interest on loans even in their sleep. The interests are charged in hours for twenty-four hours a day. If you go in for any loan the interest on it is charged in hours, so you are paying twenty-four hours multiplied by thirty-one days in a month. Therefore you should know that you are paying the interest even in your sleep. For example, you pay the interest when you visit the washroom, when you are conversing with your friend, when you attend a funeral and so on.

The interest is charged over thirty-one days in a month and it takes twenty-four hours to have one day. Your sleep has been calculated because you are being charged for thirty-one days. The rich make money when they are asleep, so if you are paying interest in your sleep, imagine how much you lose a day of your life. That is why the poor suffer paying interest on loans because they do not have systems that generate money for them in their sleep. They only make money when they are awake. If you understand the concept of multiple streams of income, you will become rich even in your sleep.

When the staff of the telecommunications networks go to work at 8a.m. and close at 5p.m., the companies still make money after working hours because people still buy credit or units and make calls. They only see the amount made the following day. If you make a call from 5p.m. to 8a.m. the following day, do you know how much the telecommunications companies are making? Do you know how many calls people make when the offices are closed?

Imagine you are twenty years old today. If since the day you were born, one Ghana cedi has been flowing into your life everyday, in one year you would have made three hundred and sixty-five Ghana cedis; in three years you would have made one thousand and ninety five Ghana cedis, meaning you would have made so much money in twenty years. Multiply your age by one Ghana cedi. If you invested this money in the first year of your life at a very low interest rate, say 10.11 per cent or 10.7 per cent, imagine the compound interest that would accrue and how much money you would make in the next twenty years at a very low interest rate. I tell you even when you are sleeping, that money will be growing for you. You must understand the concept of multiple streams of income and it will change your life story. How do you make money while you are asleep? Are you paying interest in your sleep? Is money going out of your income or coming to add to it? The rich make sure that money comes to them everyday.

The banks are making so much money. When the office is closed monies still come in because of the interest you are paying on a loan you have collected from them. You work for only eight hours and the bank has charged you for twenty-four hours, so you must work and repay the loan else you will always be in debt. How many days are there in a month? There are thirty-one days in a month and you are paying interest on a loan at the end of the month, so everyday there is a component of interest that you pay. How many hours are there in a day? There are twenty-four hours in a day. Do you work for twenty-four hours to pay the twenty-four hour loan interest?

How many hours do you work in a day? You work eight hours maximum. What do you use the rest of the hours for?

There is an interest you are paying on the loan everyday despite the fact that there are hours for sleeping, eating, dancing, drinking and so on. Divide twenty-four by three and look at the amount of money that you pay out every day of your life. The interest is too high for you because you work for only eight hours and you are paying off a loan at a twenty-four hour interest rate even when you are asleep. If you create multiple streams of income, you would probably avoid taking the loan in which case the interest would remain as part of your savings which could eventually be invested to increase the value of your investment.

The Age of Multiple Sources of Income

In the nineteen fifties it was enough for a family to have only one breadwinner because he could take care of the entire family who would live well. Those days you would hear about a housewife who took care of the house among other things but was not a wage earner. If both the husband and the wife were working, one person took care of the home with his or her money while the other saved his or her money to do other things. Couples achieved a lot in those days where one spouse's salary was able to take care of the whole family.

The family needed more than one income when it got to the nineteen seventies and the eighties because one person could not take care of the family any more. You would realize that levels of savings from the nineteen seventies to the eighties really came down. Why? The money being saved for the families could not be saved any more because incomes could no longer run the family. From the nineteen nineties to this present time, you must understand that, in some cases even two incomes cannot sustain the family. Couples may be working but they still cannot manage their family because even their two incomes put together is not sufficient for today's expenses.

Multiple Streams of Income is a concept you must understand because this is the age it is needed most. It is akin to the use of mobile phones, computer or internet by everybody now. That is what you need to use in this knowledge era and that calls for multiple streams of income else you would be left behind. The same applies to your business life. You must learn about the age we are in. Do not say you are okay where you are because whether you like it or not you must learn how to use the computer or the internet and you must use the mobile phones because this is the age you are in. The multiple streams of income is what would help you to make money to meet the demands of our era.

Bill Gates: *'This age is a very wonderful age. It is the age that knowledge is running at the speed of a thought and on a nervous digital system.'*

Your nervous system has now become digital. You cannot afford not to do it else you will pay a very huge price. The best thing is to sit up and get the understanding to get it right and it will be a bit easier for you. You must understand the multiple streams of income philosophy. You should not say to yourself that you do not need it because if you really want to survive in this age, then you need it. The age we are in is not about 'I do not want to know.' It is about 'I must know it.' It is the age of advancement that you cannot afford to ignore. You must educate yourself.

All the successful people you know are doing so many things to keep their lives going. You must know that the age that you are in is not by your choice; it is foisted on us by circumstances. In the twenty-first century, you must not joke with creating multiple streams of income. This is an age that you must not depend on your job. In the twentieth century, you could depend on your job to have satisfaction in life. But now, no one job can give you the kind of satisfaction you are looking for, so do something else your job alone cannot take you anywhere.

CHAPTER SUMMARY

Identifying and creating multiple sources of income has always been a key to making wealth. Wealthy people live by this concept even though in the beginning they may have started from a single source. Another difference between the wealthy and the poor is that the poor only make money while awake whereas the wealthy make money whether asleep or awake. If you do not understand the financial game you cannot play it. For you to play and win, you have to understand the principles that underline it.

“All riches have their origin in the mind. Wealth is in ideas – not money”.

– Robert Colhier –

”When you create multiple streams of income, you are forming a powerful tide of prosperity that can carry you along for a lifetime of fortune and freedom. And you won't only be helping yourself- friends and family will also prosper from your good fortune”.

– Robert G Allen –

CHAPTER TEN

Learn To Earn More Money

Everything that produces the right result goes through the appropriate process. As such, like all results-oriented things, the multiple streams of income should be cultivated based on certain conditions, particularly the following:

i. You must master the first stream of income

That means everybody who wants to build multiple streams of income must first build one stream of income and master it. If you do not have any stream of income or you are not doing anything productive and profitable in life, there is no way you can build multiple streams of income. You start building multiple streams of income by first finding some work to do.

Quote: *'Pursuing your passion is fulfilling and leads to financial freedom.'*

What are you passionate about in life? What are you dying for? What you are passionate about is going to be the first step in building multiple streams of income. You must build your first stream from your passion. There are so many things you must understand when working in a company. You may be working somewhere but not in your passion area. The fact that you have gone to school to master a subject chosen for you at the university level does not mean you have achieved what your passion is.

You have your passive and passion areas. You also have your passive income and your passion income so you can be working in any company but you are not passionate about what you are doing. You are working because you want to earn money to alleviate poverty. You must identify what you are passionate about at your workplace. Your first stream of income must come from an area of your passion. For some people, their passion lies in the Real Estate and for others, it is to own their own business. Your first stream of income should be something that personally excites you whether you make enough money from it or not. You just love doing it.

Every successful person would tell you that they love what they are doing. Whatever you are passionate about is not work. It is the reason why you are living. You are just energized but not irritated by it. You can do it anytime of the day or night. It flows through you naturally. This is your area of passion. You must identify your passionate area. All those who build great incomes in their lives started from their passion areas. You have more energy in your passion area. You are very strong in your passion area. If you build your area of passion, it will help you to build other areas in your life. The purpose of other streams is to make sure that your passion never dies. You create other streams of income out of your passion area because you want to keep your passion alive.

Multiple Streams of Income is about how to create residual incomes from your passion. How do you do it? Some people do not even know their passion area. You do not know what you are passionate about. You do not know how to create anything out of your passion. Moving from your passive income to passion income is a whole lot of journey. It is a whole lot of exercise. You must be able to understand how to do it. If you know how to do it, you will be excited about your life because you would become the stream.

If you create a business that becomes another stream of income for you, it means you have an additional stream of income. The good news is that you do not necessarily need to spend much of your time at the spot to produce goods or services for others. Other people can work for you everyday and the main stream, that is, the one you created the additional stream from, continuously grows stronger. You will have joy to live on this earth because you have sources that keep you going. Multiple Streams of Income is very important. It is a philosophy you must understand. Once you understand it well, your life will become better.

After completing university, most people apply for jobs which have nothing to do with the knowledge they have acquired. Most people are not really passionate about the job that they wake up very early to go and do. It is just a stepping stone to move them from where they are to where they want to be.

Research has proven that if you find yourself in any environment and you stay there for more than five years and you are not careful, you will be tuned to that environment. Most people are stuck to certain working environments because they have been there for long. They cannot move out. Whatever you are passionate about is an area you would love to stay in for long or forever. Do not run away from whatever you are doing or wherever you are for the sake of it; you can be in the same environment and build three, four or more streams of income that can give you more than you are being paid now.

For some people, when they receive their salary, the first thing that comes to mind is to buy a car or go in for a loan to build a house. If you are in your twenties you do not have to think about buying a car or building a house at that stage of your life; you must think about building multiple streams of income. You should understand what multiple streams of income is about. When you get to the next stage of your life, your streams will have stabilized to pay you more than you must have imagined. Then you can comfortably quit your job and manage your streams and you will be on top of your life.

If you do not have multiple streams of income or a stream that is paying you more than your salary, then you are not supposed to take that decision to step out of your working environment. There is one fantastic story about Abraham Lincoln when he was the President of United States of America. A certain man had an appointment to meet him at his office. Abraham Lincoln came to the reception and saw the man so he asked the secretary, *'Who is this man?'*

The Secretary said, *'He is the one looking for you.'*

Abraham Lincoln said, *'I am not ready to see this man again.'*

The Secretary asked him, *'Mr. President, why?'*

Abraham Lincoln said, *'I do not want to see him again.'*

The Secretary asked him again, *'Why?'*

He said, *'I do not like his face at all.'*
The Secretary was so surprised and so she asked the President, *'Mr. President, you do not like the*

face of the man but he is coming to see you?'

He said, *'No, I do not like his face because every man is responsible for his face after age forty and I do not like the look on this man's face.'*

What Abraham Lincoln means is that if after forty years, the man cannot treat his face very well, cannot smile but looks as if the whole world is about to fall on him, he is not ready to associate with him. There is going to be a certain time in your life that age will fight you. At that point you should have what it takes to match age in terms of all the things that the age fight will present to oppose you.

Wisdom quote: *'Money may not buy happiness but it surely helps one look for it in more interesting places.'*

An English proverb concerning Multiple Streams of Income: *'With money in your pocket you are wise, you are handsome and you sing well too.'*

ii. You must build a system with the first income

You must systematize your first stream of income. You must put a system in place to the extent that your absence will not be felt because your stream would still produce for you. You must use two things to get that system. The most difficult part of it is **building the stream** and **making it a system.**

Your stream would become a system through the application called **Time Leverage.** Time leverage is getting all the necessary things in place so you can have **Human Employees.** You make your stream a system by employing somebody to handle it for you.

The second one is called the **Technology Leverage,** which refers to **Digital Employees.**

You must have time that human beings must handle. You should be able to master these two before building another stream. If you do not master them and you build another stream, it will be difficult for it to work.

How do you master the first stream? Most people do not like to build the system because they think if they put in people, their streams will be destroyed by the people. Having others to work with you or for you helps to leverage your time. You must master these skills so that your first stream can run on **autopilot.** If you do not master the time and technology leverage, that first stream cannot get to the autopilot stage.

The autopilot stage is when your stream has become stable because you can now make **residual income.** Residual income is an income that flows into your life even in your absence and without your physical efforts. On the other hand, if you want to build a stream from your passion, you must be physically present. At least you must have eighty per cent presence there. Your heart, mind and body must be there. You spend all your life in building it. When you have spare time, you build it.

When you finish you put a system around it by trying as much as possible to leverage your time and technology. These two elements of your system would achieve the autopilot stage for you to enjoy your residual income and cash flow. When you get to the traffic light, for example, there is nobody there but the light will indicate red, amber or green. Red tells you to stop. Nobody is there but technology is working. The traffic light is a technology leverage. It does not need any human being to be there. The time is controlled and that is how it is. You must be able to leverage time and technology.

One advantage of multiple streams of income is that if you lose your job, your income would reduce but would not disappear. This means the stream will be able to support you even when you are jobless and even if the support is insufficient it is better than not having anything at all. At least you can meet some financial obligations like paying bills.

Any time we think of multiple streams of income we should think of financial goals too. The financial goal can be for five years (medium term goal) or ten years (long term). The multiple streams of income helps us to achieve our financial goals faster to give us financial freedom.

Financial freedom is achieved when you no longer need your job to cover your living expenses. Financial freedom gives you greater flexibility and leverage. You are in a much more powerful position when you know that you are not hundred per cent(100%) dependent on your job. For some of us, our life is dependent on our jobs. You cannot depend hundred per cent on your job; it is very risky.

Multiple streams of income is not necessarily a better business or a better job. It is a concept that helps you to be able to live and live well because it gives that financial leverage. Multiple streams of income is about how you make money work for you without you exerting any energy in most cases or just use infinitesimal amount of energy. It means you use all your energies and time somewhere else to get your first income but other sources of income should give you money without you sweating for it. It should be like a windfall.

If you are thinking of financial freedom but have hundred per cent dependency on your current job, it will get to a certain stage in your life when you will be very sorry.

Mark Twain: *'A banker is a fellow who lends you his umbrella when the sun is shining and wants it back the minute it begins to rain.'*

Margaret Thatcher: *'No one will remember the Good Samaritan if he had only had good intentions, he had money as well.'*

Leonard Osborn: *'Unless you try to do something beyond what you have already mastered, you will never grow.'*

Quote: *'A banker is somebody who charges you high interest to lend you somebody else's money.'*

iii. You must learn how to leverage resources to create additional stream

You must be able to create more streams based on the concept you used to create the first stream. It is very important. Most people are very successful in creating the first stream in their passion area but they cannot create the system around it. The business must be a system. If you are not able to do the second one, then you cannot create another stream out of it. If you are not able to master the first stream of income, then there is no way for you to try the second one.

Some people say that they have tried it several times but it did not work. It is not that it did not work but they did not do it well. It is a concept that they must understand. It is not like just getting up and starting a business because somebody said you should do it. Everybody wants something to be run for him or her. I know so many people who have tried certain businesses which did not work and because of that they have relaxed. It is more risky to take that stance.

If you want to succeed in life, you must learn how to take risk and if you want to take a risk you must learn how to minimize your risk. How do you minimize risk? You minimize the risk by learning about it. This way you would grow and get on well. How do you grow and become better if you do not learn? The multiple stream of income is a concept that should be understood. It cannot be practised suddenly. It is something you have to sit down and learn about before you take the first step for it.

If you want to make a residual income, then you must get a strong system. Do you believe you can cook rice better than the Papaye Restaurant? Have you made a system out of it? When I ask this question in seminars, I get a very good response from the audience and they realize that they can do better but Papaye is making more money because its owner has been able to create a system around it. He has turned his cooking into business.

Some of us want to do something but we cannot turn it to become a business. We cannot systematize it and if you can not, how does it become a business? Some people can do so many things but they cannot systematize them. You must systematize what you do and master it before you can move on to the next one that gives you the leverage to get additional income. You must think about how to leverage your skills and knowledge and also network.

The first stream of income that you created was able to benefit certain people because they started working with you and enjoying from it. These same people can be used to build your second stream of income. If you can create one stream of income every year, just ask yourself how many streams of income you are going to create in the next five years? You can have five streams of income in the next five years. If you can create one stream of income every six months, just imagine the number in two years. You can create four streams of income.

The first stream of income is what you must master and if you are able to systematize it, it makes it a bit easier to build additional streams of income. If it took you two or three years to master the first stream of income, the second stream will take you less, probably one year and the third one will take you about six months and so on. It is so because now you know how to do it.

You must take the first step and do it and the rest will become easy for you. That is why there are people creating more businesses and it is easier for them to create the additional businesses. Why do you think they can create businesses very easily and you can not do it? It is because they have done it and they have been able to pay the price of the first one to do the second, the third and so on.

Multiple streams of income is very important for you to understand because if you do not understand it at this age, it is going to be very difficult for you to take the challenge and responsibility to try something with your life. You can start something with two hundred Ghana cedis or one hundred Ghana cedis. You can save some money between now and the end of the year and start something but get more ideas and knowledge while you wait to start that stream.

Multiple streams of income is a concept you can practise at your own will. You must do it to be able to help you move on with your life. Once you understand multiple streams of income, you can leverage resources to get additional streams of income. Each person must be able to create more streams of income because the average person can do five different things and do them very well. As long as you are living on this earth, there are five things you can do and do them very well. That is why some people have created more businesses. Recently the owner of Zoom Lion, a waste management company, was reported to have created about thirty-four businesses and he is running all of them. There are people who have ten streams, fourteen streams and even more. What do you have to do? You must be able to understand the concept and once you understand it, it becomes a bit easier to move on.

Quote: *'When a man tells you that he got rich through hard work ask him whose?'*

Everybody is working very hard but you must be able to understand how to work very well. If you want to enjoy your future, then you must start today to understand the concept of the multiple streams of income. Once you understand it, it makes it a bit easier for you. Try as much as possible to build at least one stream of income before the year ends. People have restaurants which make money for them even in their absence. That is why Richard Branson has created over two hundred businesses and he is able to manage all of them. Why? He understands the concept, based upon which he has been able to create more businesses.

How do you leverage your time? How do you leverage technology? How do you build multiple streams of income? How do you develop yourself? How do you get on with your life? How do you transform your life? How do you move on and get the best out of your life?

Robert Allan: *'When you create multiple streams of income you are forming a powerful tide of prosperity that can carry you along for a lifetime of fortune and freedom and you would not only be helping yourself, friends and family will also prosper from your own fortune.'*

Once you understand the concept of multiple streams of income, you are really creating a very powerful tide of prosperity. If you want to prosper you must first of all learn how to make it and you will be blessed to get on with what you are doing. If you do not understand what multiple streams of income is, it means you are not prepared to be serious with your life. It is a concept that every successful person on this earth has studied and has clear understanding of how it works.

CHAPTER SUMMARY

The first step is to have a stream of income before you can have a multiple streams of income. That first stream must be something that personally excites you whether you make enough money from it or not. Multiple streams of income is not necessarily a better business or a better job; it is a concept that helps you to be able to live well because of the financial leverage it offers. With the multiple streams of income, when you lose one source, your income will reduce but it will not disappear.

"If you could be wealthy, think of saving as well as getting".

– Benjamin Franklin –

"A penny saved is a penny earned"

– Benjamin Franklin –

CHAPTER ELEVEN

The Strength Of The One Ghana Cedi

Imagine you have a stream that gives you a profit of one Ghana cedi everyday. Do you think it is easy to make one Ghana cedi? It is not. The multiple streams of income is not about getting up to go into business. You can do your own business or work with any organization because it is about developing something out of your passion. You can work in any organization, and create a stream that can generate some income in your absence. If you are being paid X amount every month and you also make a profit of one Ghana cedi a day from a stream you have built, how much will you make at the end of the month from that stream? You will make thirty Ghana cedis and if that amount is generated for a year, how much money will you make? If that stream exists for two years, how much will you make?

If you have one stream of income that generates one Ghana cedi a day and you have been able to create five of such streams, how much are you making every day? You will make five Ghana cedis a day. You can be working in any organization but that one Ghana cedi that you make everyday will change your life story. If you have a stream that makes thirty Ghana cedis every day and you buy something at the cost of fifty Ghana cedis in a day, your stream will be able to pay half of that amount.

Multiple streams of income is about helping you to make an extra income that will make you feel free and able to enjoy the best out of your life. It is a concept that helps you to generate money in your absence. Creating multiple streams of income can have a major impact on your finance. If you have an extra income every month, just imagine the kind of impact it will make in your life. If you have any business that gives you profit of one Ghana cedi every day, you will understand the concept of multiple streams of income.

Multiple streams of income is a basic concept that teaches you how any extra money you earn, even interest on savings, can work for you. How does interest work for you? How do you create a stream that can generate extra income? Does interest flow out of you or to you. If you owe somebody and you are paying interest that means interest is 'coming out of you'. If somebody owes you and the money is being paid plus interest, that means you have money flowing to you. In the multiple streams of income, you have to understand that money must work for you and not against you, and that is the interest you earn.

You must understand interest for it to work for you. The rich know how interest works for them but interest works against you because it comes out of you. When interest gets out of you, how do you become successful? You can never become successful if interest is going out of you; you can only become successful when interest is coming to you even when you are asleep. That is why Multiple Streams of Income teaches you how money can make more money for you (that is residual income) while you are even at your office. Residual income is the money you will make in your absence. You put systems together and they will work very well for you.

It has been proven that ninety-five per cent (95%) of all success comes from the system and not people. That is why any productive thing you are doing needs a system for it to be able to make more money for you. You can have great businesses running for you but if you do not know how to put a system around them, they would not do well. If you know how to cook kenkey, for instance, and you are able to systematize it, you will see success. If you are able to generate just one

Ghana cedi a day for a whole year, you would be able to accumulate three hundred and sixty-five Ghana cedis.

If you are pregnant now, put one Ghana cedi aside every day for the baby you are carrying and continue when it is born. When the child is ten years, you can check how much money you have accumulated for him. Then you will know how powerful one Ghana cedi every day is. That is why there is a saying that 'little drops of water make a mighty ocean.' Any system generating one Ghana cedi for you will change your life story. How much money do you need to generate one Ghana cedi? What can you do to get one Ghana cedi? Some of you have space, you have friends, and so many people around you, so if you can easily generate one Ghana cedi every day and systematize it, you will be a successful person in a very short time.

All that you know now is what you are doing. How much you are being paid at the end of the month. That is where your interest lies. If you have a system that generates just one Ghana cedi every day for you and even you lose that job, you will see how important that one Ghana cedi is. If you are able to keep that money and grow it, that money will be able to build a great mansion for you one day and if you create more streams you will get more of the one Ghana cedi. If at the end of the day, one Ghana cedi is coming from twenty different streams just imagine how your life is going to be like.

Put in place a system that will generate one Ghana cedi for you everyday for investment and the creation of multiple streams of income.

CHAPTER SUMMARY

If you have one stream of income that generates one Ghana cedi a day, and you are able to create five of such streams, you can imagine how much you will make in a day, a month, a year or even a decade. Multiple streams of income is about helping you to make an extra income that will cushion your life. Saving one Ghana cedi a day would help you generate three hundred and sixty five Ghana cedis in a year and that is enough capital to start a new business. Create a system that can generate one Ghana cedi everyday for you to invest in other ventures.

"How many millionaires do you know who have become wealthy by investing in savings accounts? I rest my case".

– Anne Wilson Schaef –

"Influence is like a savings account. The less you use it, the more you've got".

– Andrew Young –

CHAPTER TWELVE

No Answer In Savings Account

Savings Account

It is very important to have savings account. If you intend to earn two thousand five hundred Ghana cedis a month from the savings account at four per cent(4%) interest per annum, for example, then you need to save seven hundred and sixty-five thousand Ghana cedis. You can see how much money you need to save before you can make this amount. Do you have that money to save to achieve that target? No, savings cannot make you become successful because you need to save so much before you can make that little. Even you need an interest of four per cent(4%) before you can make two thousand five hundred Ghana cedis a month on that big principal.

Investment Account

If you have an investment account, for instance, and you want to earn about thirty thousand Ghana cedis from your investment account at ten per cent (10%) interest per annum, you need to invest about three hundred thousand Ghana cedis.

If you understand the multiple streams of income, it makes it a bit easier. This is because if you can make that two thousand five hundred Ghana cedis per month from any business or two hundred Ghana cedis every month from any stream of income you create, for instance, this can help you meet a lot of the financial obligations in your life. It can help you start something great. A small amount as an extra income can go a long way to turn your life around.

Be in that organization but learn how to create another and extra income, however small it is. The little extra income that you are making can change something in your life for the better.

Get this concept of multiple streams of income because all successful people understand this concept. That is why the richest man in the world, Carlos Slim, has a number of streams of income. There are so many such businessmen in this country and they are creating more streams. Capital 02 is now selling water but you know its original stream was medicine. Make sure you will create another stream that can generate at least one Ghana cedi a day for you to change the story of your life. Do you now have an idea about how to generate one Ghana cedi? If you have an idea, you can change your story.

Rudy Allen: *'If only God will give me some clear sign like making a deposit in my name, in a Swiss bank account.'*

Multiple streams of income help you to diversify your efforts and your talent. If you lose one stream of income, you have others to fall on. The reason you must rush to build multiple streams of income has to do with the economy. There is no stable economy anywhere in the world. Anything can happen in any country to negatively affect the economy. People have lost so many things in life because of the instability of their economies. What happened in the U.S economy from 2005 – 2009 affected everybody in the world.

The economy of any country can get worse or better. The only thing that can help you to be able to move on with your life is the concept of multiple streams of income. If you understand the concept you will be able to stand anything that happens to the economy. If the unexpected happens to any economy, it will have effect on businesses and so you need the multiple streams to absorb all the economic shocks. If you have multiple streams of income, what happens is that if it gets worse, for instance, and affects a number of your streams of income, you would have others to keep you running and to help to put back on track those streams that were blown off by the crises.

Any time you complain that the economy is not doing well, other businesses are doing well. It does not affect every business. You will feel the economy when things do not go well. When a major downturn hit the economy in the world, so many things happened. When things are not going well, you will not feel it much once your multiple streams of income are working for you.

Warren Buffet: *'It's only when the tide goes out that you can see who is naked.'*

The reason why you have to be serious with creating the multiple streams of income is that the economic trends in the 21st century call for that practice. We are in the age of multiple streams of income due to the economic crises in the world and that concept has become the only means that helps you to excel in life.

No country has a stable economy and no country will ever have one. World economies go up and down. Because of the instability of economies in the world, the only thing that can make you stable is the multiple streams of income.

Any time the economy becomes unstable some businesses will be affected but the beautiful thing is that when the economy is not stable or when there is instability in the economy (economic crises), it does not affect all businesses. The effect of the crises will depend on the kind of crises that the economy is going through. Sometimes you wonder why some are complaining about the economy while others are not. Those complaining see the crises and seriously get affected by them because their single sources of income become devastated. If you have multiple streams of income and there is any economic crisis, it affects some of your streams but not all. Those not affected will be able to help the ones which have been affected to stand in the course of time.

Multiple streams of income is a concept that will help you balance your life if you understand it. That is why you need to create more of the streams for you to be able to stand the tide. It is not about whether or not you want to do it; you have to do it so you will be able to stand in times of economic crises. You must understand the concept and create some streams for yourself. You must understand the concept of multiple streams of income because it gives financial freedom.

CHAPTER SUMMARY

Having other sources of income helps you to diversify your talents and master other trade to your own benefit. In a world where economic stability is not guaranteed and many people are losing their capital, your versatility in the world of work is what will sustain you. Do not allow economic trends to negatively affect your life and business. Develop other sources of income and insure your life against economic instability.

"It's difficult to get a man to understand something if his salary depends upon he not understanding it".

– Upton Sinclair –

"A wise man should have money in his head, but not in his heart.

– Jonathan Swift –

CHAPTER THIRTEEN

The Payday Life

If you are living a life of *'payday'* or a life where you talk about money only at the end of the month, then you must think of multiple streams of income. There are so many people whose lives are seriously affected when there are delays in the payment of salaries because all their lives have been programmed and fixed on their salaries. Everything about them is about their salaries. Most of their discussions are about their salaries; nothing more, nothing less.

If your life is totally run on your salary it is very dangerous. Imagine what will happen to you if you lose your job. It is going to be disastrous during all the period you would live without a job. If all you depend on is your pay, and so that is what you have hung the lives of your children on, then their future is in jeopardy. Paydays become so important to you that if people play with your *'payday'* you would hang them but for the laws of the country. If you owe someone, all that you tell the person is that *'at the end of the month, I will pay you.'* Any time you talk to somebody about your indebtedness all you say is that 'I will give you the money at the end of the month.' That has become your lifestyle and so the common question that you keep asking is *'when are we going to be paid?'* Immediately you receive your salary, you begin to think about when the next salary is going to come. If you are that kind of person, you are living a dangerous life because the day you lose your job, everybody will know it earlier than it should be.

Your life is in danger, so you must understand the concept of the multiple streams of income. If you understand the multiple streams of income that burden will be off your neck for you to live a comfortable life, which is the kind of life you are supposed to live on this earth, not one dependent on your pay.

Most of us live a 'payday' life, where we wish we can forward the days in the month for us to receive the next salary earlier than it should be. If you have a mentality that every day should be a payday, then you are not ready to be counted among successful people. It is a poverty mentality to think only about when you are going to receive your next wage or pay.

You can break that mentality by applying the concept of multiple streams of income. Once you find yourself at that level, you must make a conscious effort to move away from that mentality and to build a mentality where you will have a secured life, a life of financial freedom. It means that you are not financially free so you need to build a life of financial freedom where you can live comfortably with or without your pay because you have other sources of income.

Delays in payment of salaries are big issues for you. You can fight the organization because the accountant did not pay you on time. We know so many people who, because of delays in payment of salaries, have picked so many issues with their employers because their lives are being threatened. You must change that attitude by doing all you can to understand the concept of multiple streams of income and practise it.

CHAPTER SUMMARY

A life that is totally run on salary is a life heading towards an abyss. All hope and budget is hung on it and so the day or month you lose your job your world comes crushing. Most of us live a 'payday life', where we wish we can forward the days in the month for us to receive the next salary earlier than expected. If you have a mentality that every day should be a 'payday', then you are not ready to be counted among successful people.

"The person who doesn't know where his next dollar is coming from usually doesn't know where his last dollar went".

– Unknown –

"What we really want to do is what we really meant to do , when we do what we are meant to do, money comes to us , doors open for us, we feel useful, and the work we do feels like play to us".

– Julia Cameron –

CHAPTER FOURTEEN

Spring From Your First Income

Since the concept of Multiple Streams Of Income is concerned with income generation, you need to know the three types of income, namely Earned , Portfolio and Passive Incomes.

i. Earned Income

If your life is the payday kind, that means you live on 'the earned income,' which is the money that you have worked for. This kind of income usually cannot keep you and your home running. You cannot depend on the earned income where you exchange your time for money. You are really exchanging your life for money and you become aggressive when after 'giving' your life, your employer delays in giving you your salary. “Yes, I have worked for it and I must earn it”, you may say.

If your life is hooked to earned income, it is a dangerous situation. You must sit up because that kind of life will not help you. If you are living that kind of life, even harmless things would make you to be annoyed and that is why you fight with everybody in your life. “I do not play with my pay,” you would say. Yes, we know you do not play with your pay, but how long can you live at that?

You have got slogans or words that drive you because your life is dependent on your pay. If that is how you are living your life, please it is a dangerous life. Just ask yourself what would happen if you fall sick and you do not go to work for two months. Just imagine if you become bed-ridden for three years, how will you run your life? If what you are making at the end of the month is all that you depend on, then if anything bad happens to you, your situation can be anybody's guess. How are you going to live the rest of your life?

You must understand the concept of multiple streams of income and generate or create another stream so that if one stops flowing, the other will flow. Do not live your life on earned income. Earning income is very good but that should not be a do-or-die issue such that if you do not receive your salary on time, then your world has come to an end.

Your earned income should be a springboard for making more money. Therefore spring from your first income whether it is a monthly wage or earning from that small business.

ii. Portfolio Income

Successful people do not live on earned income; they live on portfolio income. They use the earned income to create another income called the portfolio income. Portfolio income refers to the paper asset income such as the stock, the fixed deposit, bonds and the treasury bills.

These people work and save some of their incomes to buy stocks in organizations. They have fixed deposits, bonds and treasury bills; they have created other streams of income. In case of any eventuality, they know what to fall on, where to go and what to do. You must move away from the earned income to the portfolio income by selecting all or some of the different kinds of portfolio. Multiple streams of income teaches you how to make a portfolio income.

iii. Passive Income

Successful people make another kind of income called passive income. Passive income comes from investment in things like real estate and writing of books.

Successful people make money not from their earned income but from their portfolio and passive incomes. The rich and the middle class make their monies from these kinds of income. They use their earned income to create portfolio and passive incomes because they cannot depend on their earned income.

The money you are being paid cannot take care of you but that money can create another income that can take care of you. How do you generate, grow or try as much as possible to build something that can keep you going? Do not depend on your pay. Use it to create another income and depend on that one rather.

Somebody says the money he earns is just from hand to mouth. If it is from hand to mouth, squeeze the one that goes into your mouth and leave some in your hand. If you put all in your mouth you will swallow it and your stomach will become full, only for you to run to the 'exit point.' Keep some in your hand. Do not be a payday person. Do not depend on your earned income.

No successful person depends on earned income. Successful people depend on their streams. You do not have to leave your place of work. Multiple streams of income is a concept and technology. It does not tell you to leave your place of work. You must work there because that is your primary source of income. You use that place to create another source and continue to create more streams. Do not be that person who receives his or her salary, and all he or she does is to spend all the money and wait for another payday. The first person to turn the calendar to the new month is you. You want to check when you are going to receive your next salary. That should not be your lifestyle. If you live that kind of life, you can never have financial independence.

Multiple streams of income teaches you how to create portfolio and passive incomes from your earned income. There are some small businesses you can start. How do you generate money from the stock? How do you try to turn your money around? Get income from portfolio and passive incomes and that can help you to have a better life. It does not matter how much you are being paid. If you live your life on the money that you are being paid, you will come back to point zero. You must not depend on your earned income but on your portfolio and passive incomes.

Get a portfolio stream and strive for a passive income. Make money from passive and portfolio incomes. If you depend on your earned income, you will become somebody who is always waiting for the payday.

CHAPTER SUMMARY

If you live on an 'earned income', then your life is solely dependent on your salary. This kind of income cannot keep you and your home running. You must move away from the 'earned income' to the 'portfolio income', which refers to the paper asset income such as stock and bonds. Successful people make money not from their 'earned income' but from their portfolio and passive incomes which are usually earnings from long-term investment like real estate and writing of books. Build your world around the right source of income and be seen at the top.

"Success is not to be pursued; It is to be attracted by the person you become."

– Jim Rohn –

" Don't wish it were easier; wish you were better. Don't wish for less problems; wish for more skills. Don't wish for less challenges; wish for more wisdom."

– Jim Rohn –

"Don't let someone else's opinion of you become your reality."

– Les Brown –

CHAPTER FIFTEEN

Conclusion

Every tree of poverty planted in your house has been uprooted in the name of Jesus. All stagnant water in your house or your life that smells has all been cleared in the name of Jesus. All the cool water in your life that is making your life cool has all been removed in the name of Jesus. Every rope that has been used to tie you down so that you can't move forward and that has made you believe that you or your family cannot go far has been broken in pieces in the name of Jesus. Get rid of the slavery that is in your mind. Henceforth, deliver yourself from the slavery of your mind. Some women have accepted the fact that they can't give birth. Know that if there is any slavery in your mind, you can't get anything good neither can you create any wealth. Pray and ask God to give you the strength to control your mind. From now on, everything that is wealth-attracting would be in your mind.

Present your bodies as a living sacrifice, holy and acceptable unto God, which is your reasonable service. Moreover, may you be transformed by the renewing of your mind that you may prove what is good, acceptable and perfect will of God. The Bible commands us to renew our mind and we must do exactly so.

Change that mindset and tell your body, “I am becoming rich; for God created me to be rich.” If you are praying and your mind tells you that you are tired, tell your mind that the Bible says, “I should pray without ceasing”, so I should not be tired of praying. Recreate your life. Tell yourself that everything you do would prosper and that it shall be well with your children also in Jesus’name.

Do not accept it that you are sick, change your mindsct. You would build your own housc in thc name of Jesus. You would buy your own car in the name of Jesus. Remember that everything comes from the mind. You shall not be the tail, but the head. The Heavens are open for you, so create your own wealth.

Cast out any mindset that does not tally with the word of God. The mindset that hinders your financial, business and marital progress should be cast out in the mighty name of Jesus. Henceforth ask that the mind of God comes and stays in you. Let the word and the Spirit of God dwell richly in you. Now, say " I am free forever in Jesus' name."

Thank God you have enjoyed reading this book.

A-M-E-N

CHAPTER SUMMARY

Know that you can't create wealth with an

enslaved mind. Pray and ask God to give you strength to control your mind. Discard any mindset that does not tally with the word of God. You were born to be successful and so you must work believing that God has His eyes on you and your business.